YOU CHOOSE
BOOKS ™

AT BATTLE IN
WORLD WAR I

AN INTERACTIVE BATTLEFIELD ADVENTURE

by Allison Lassieur

Consultant:
Dennis P. Mroczkowski
Colonel, U.S. Marine Corps Reserve (Retired)
Williamsburg, Virginia

CAPSTONE PRESS
a capstone imprint

You Choose Books are published by Capstone Press,
1710 Roe Crest Drive, North Mankato, Minnesota 56003
www.capstonepub.com

Library of Congress Cataloging-in-Publication Data
Lassieur, Allison.
  At battle in World War I : an interactive battlefield adventure / by Allison Lassieur.
    pages cm. — (You choose books. You choose: battlefields)
  Includes bibliographical references and index.
  Summary: "In You Choose format, explores World War I through the eyes of sailors,
pilots, and infantry soldiers on the frontline"—Provided by publisher.
  ISBN 978-1-4914-2151-2 (library binding)
  ISBN 978-1-4914-2393-6 (paperback)
  ISBN 978-1-4914-2397-4 (eBook PDF)
1. World War, 1914–1918—Juvenile literature. 2. Plot-your-own stories. I. Title.
  D522.7.L37 2014
  940.4—dc23   2014024322

Editorial Credits
Mari Bolte, editor; Tracy Davies McCabe and Charmaine Whitman, designers;
Wanda Winch, media researcher; Laura Manthe, production specialist

Printed in Canada.
092014   008478FRS15

TABLE OF CONTENTS

4

ABOUT YOUR ADVENTURE

World War I (1914–1918) changed the way wars were fought. The modern tools of war invented then have stood the passage of time. Many are still in use today.

In this book you'll explore the choices people made. You'll also learn about the new technology used to win the war. The events, situations, and battles you'll experience happened to real people.

Chapter One sets the scene. Then you choose which path to read. Follow the directions at the bottom of each page. The choices you make will change your outcome. After you finish one path, go back and read the others for new perspectives and more adventures.

YOU CHOOSE the path
you take through history.

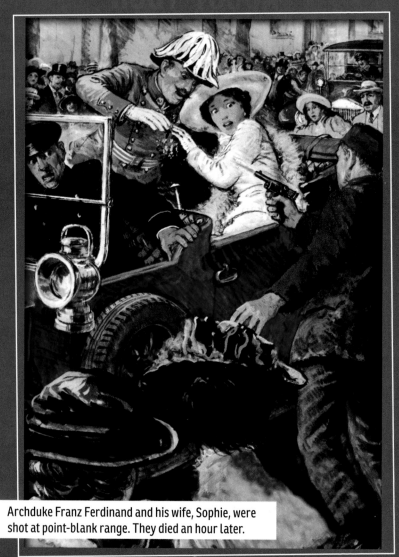

Archduke Franz Ferdinand and his wife, Sophie, were shot at point-blank range. They died an hour later.

1

BLOOD ON THE
BATTLEFIELD

It was called the War to End All Wars—the first global war in the history of the world. World War I spanned across Europe, Africa, the Middle East, and over the oceans.

A single event led to the war. In 1914 the heir to the Austro-Hungarian throne, Archduke Franz Ferdinand, was assassinated. The killer was a Serb named Gavrilo Princip. His actions led Austria-Hungary to declare war on Serbia. Most of the world thought the war would only be between those two countries.

Turn the page.

But then Serbia asked Russia to help it fight. France had promised to help Russia. Great Britain joined the war to help France. They formed the Allied Powers, known as the Allies.

Austria-Hungary asked Germany for help. Along with the Ottoman Empire, they formed the Central Powers. In just a few months, a small war had become a global conflict.

Europe 1915

New weapons made this war terrifying. Flamethrowers, tanks, airplanes, machine guns, submarines, and chemical warfare were used for the first time. As the battles grew, so did each country's weapons technology. Sometimes countries stole ideas from each other.

You are a young man ready to do your part. There are many ways to serve and protect your country. Which will you choose?

To use the new invention of airplanes as a British pilot, turn to page 11.

To fight in the Allied trenches with the latest artillery and tanks, turn to page 45.

To be a sailor on powerful British ships and submarines, turn to page 77.

Zeppelins could fly higher and farther than airplanes. They could stay in the air for 24 hours and reach speeds of 78 miles per hour.

②
WAR IN
THE AIR

World War I started a year ago, in 1914. It began far away in Austria-Hungary. You're not too sure how it started. All you know is that your country, Great Britain, is fighting alongside Russia and France. Germany and other countries are the enemy.

One day a shadow passes over your London home. It is Germany's most terrifying weapon: the zeppelin. Each huge airship carries up to two tons of explosives. Bombs have been dropped on Great Britain since early 1915. Buildings, streets, and houses are destroyed in these air raids. The sight of a zeppelin sends everyone into a panic.

Turn the page.

Great Britain has no way to defend against the huge ships. You are tired of sitting around waiting to be bombed. You are 18 and you want to join the war—in order to help end it. Early one morning you go to a recruiting station. After a medical exam, the officer asks, "Interested in the Royal Flying Corps?"

The Royal Flying Corps accepted men between the ages of 18 and 30.

Airplanes are a newer invention. You've never seen one up close. Your heart leaps with excitement.

"Are you single?" the officer asks. "Flying is dangerous, and we don't take married men." You assure him that you are not married, but his warning makes you nervous.

"Brilliant!" the officer says. "We use airplanes for reconnaissance. They watch the enemy and report on troop and artillery locations. Two men fly in each airplane. The pilot flies the plane. The observer takes photographs and makes notes. Both are important." The officer wants to know which you'd like to do.

13

To train as an observer, turn to page 14.

To train as a pilot, turn to page 19.

Aerial photographs were timed to slightly overlap. Then all the photos were put together like a puzzle.

You are the first one to volunteer to be an observer. Some of the other recruits look at you like you are crazy. But you know not everyone can be a pilot, and the idea of using a camera for the first time is exciting in its own way. The first portable camera, the Brownie, came out in 1900, but you've never used one.

A few days later you find yourself at a training camp in the countryside.

"Let's get one thing straight," the training officer begins. "Pilots fly the plane. Your job is every bit as important. The photographs you take will help the army locate the enemy's position, artillery, and troop movements."

Training lasts several months. You study enemy troops and how they move. You learn what various artillery weapons look like from the air.

You finally learn how to use a camera. The cameras are huge. Yours is as tall as your hip and weighs 75 pounds.

The photos you take will be lined up to form one big picture called a mosaic map. Specially trained photo interpreters will study the photos to look for clues on the enemy's position. It takes as little as 20 minutes for your photos to be developed and printed.

Turn the page.

It's exciting to be part of the aerial photography team. Pilots and photographers working together can gather six times more intelligence than traditional cavalry units in the same amount of time. You begin to think that maybe you can make a difference in the war.

You've been waiting to get in the air. It's time to prove yourself.

One day the training officer asks for volunteers. It's time for the first training flights. Are you ready?

To volunteer, go to page 17.

To wait your turn, turn to page 31.

The morning is bright and clear. The sun is soothing, but it doesn't help your nervous stomach. Your pilot is a young man named James. He sees the look on your face.

"Don't worry, chap," he says cheerfully. "I've had a whole five hours of solo flight training!" The plane is a tiny two-seater with double wings. Its seats are open to the air and are barely big enough for you and your equipment.

James leaps into the cockpit and adjusts his goggles. They are just like the ones you are wearing, along with a heavy leather coat and a leather helmet. The fur-lined goggles will protect your face from the cold wind thousands of feet above the ground.

The mechanic tries to start the plane by pushing the propeller. Nothing happens. He curses and tries again.

Turn the page.

Black smoke begins to pour from the engine. You ask James what would happen if this happened in the sky. He shrugs.

"We die," he says. "We all have to die sometime. But better to die here than at home in an air raid, am I right? Let's face our fears head on, like knights of the sky!"

The first planes were made of wood, cloth, and wire. Their top speed was only around 70 miles per hour.

18

To reconsider, turn to page 33.

To stay in the plane, turn to page 34.

On the first day of training, the new recruits gather on a grassy field. The sun glints off of the line of shiny airplanes. It's hard to believe you will soon be flying one.

"Today everyone gets to go up on a demonstration flight," the instructor says. "Who wants to go first?"

The first group of volunteers jumps into the front seats of the small two-seater planes. Pilots slide into their assigned planes. One by one the planes roar across the field and into the air. Each pilot circles the field a few times and then makes a bumpy landing. One plane looks to be having trouble. The pilot can't seem to keep the wings level while in the air.

Everything else seems to freeze in time as you watch the plane take a nosedive and crash.

To take your flight, turn to page 20.

To change your mind, turn to page 37.

You watch numbly as people rush to the wreckage. Dozens of hands pull the pilot and the recruit from the debris. Neither man is moving. They are quickly taken away on stretchers.

Mechanics and other personnel appear and start cleaning up the wreck. But it's right back to business for the remaining recruits. The training officer looks at you. "Your turn," he says. "If you're not afraid, that is."

Backing out seems like the best choice, but you don't want the other men to think you're a coward. So you tell yourself that one crash is not going to change your mind. Before you realize what's happening, you're in the seat. The plane rises into the sky. You're flying! The world and its problems seem far away. By the time your plane makes a safe landing, you're hooked.

Training lasts for weeks. You learn how to recognize the landscape and use roads and railroads as guides. You barely pay attention to the brief classes about how the plane's engine works. Your instructor says that the less a pilot knows about the plane the better.

Later you hear him tell another instructor that if a pilot doesn't know anything about engines, and he gets a bad plane, he'll fly it anyway because he doesn't know the difference. You decide to start paying more attention to how the planes stay in the air.

Everyone gets basic training on taking off, landing, and how to steer the plane in the air. Each day you fly a little longer. After just eight hours of flying time, training is over. You're officially a pilot!

Turn the page.

Your plane is a beauty, a BE2. It has two seats and can reach heights of 10,000 feet. It can carry enough fuel to stay in the air for about three hours. The other seat holds either an observer or bombs, but not both. The BE2 does not have any guns—guns are too heavy for this aircraft. Also, there is no way to fire a gun through the spinning propeller.

The day after your last lesson, orders come through. You're going to the Western Front in France. A big battle is coming.

The airfield is near a small French village about 20 miles behind the front lines. All the pilots in your squadron live here. Cows graze peacefully in the fields nearby. It's so peaceful you can hardly believe there's a war going on.

The officer commanding the Royal Flying Corps in France is Hugh Trenchard. He was one of the first commanders to use cameras instead of sketching what they saw. Because of his loud voice, Trenchard's nickname is "Boom"—but you know better than to call him that to his face.

"We are starting a big offensive against the German army," he tells his pilots. "The Royal Flying Corps will have an important part to play in the Battle of Loos." He unrolls a huge map.

Hugh Trenchard (center) was known as the Father of the Royal Air Force.

Turn the page.

"It's going to be our largest attack campaign this year," he continues, outlining the battle site as he talks. "We have more fighters and more supplies than the enemy. We're going to attack with artillery, then with gas, and then we'll storm the trenches."

"I need pilots for reconnaissance missions, and I need bombers. Who's in?"

To go on the reconnaissance mission, go to page 25.

To go on the bombing mission, turn to page 29.

You've gone through several practice missions, but now it's time for the real thing. Your mission is to locate and map enemy positions. The maps will give the artillery their targets for the coming battle. You and the observer, Frank, meet at the airplane before dawn. He loads his camera and sketchpad and climbs aboard. You hand him a pistol.

"What's this for?" he asks.

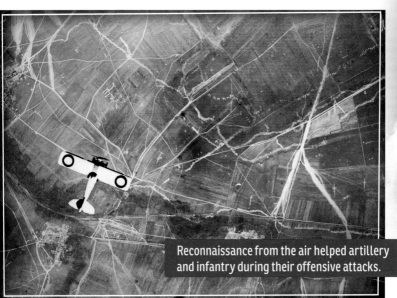

Reconnaissance from the air helped artillery and infantry during their offensive attacks.

Turn the page.

"This plane doesn't have any guns," you explain. "If we get shot at by the Germans, use the revolver to shoot back. And you'll want it if the airplane catches fire while we're flying."

Frank doesn't understand.

"There is no way to survive if the airplane catches fire," you explain. "We are not allowed to wear parachutes. We're supposed to stay with the plane." Frank turns white at this grim news.

"Besides," you say, giving him a friendly punch on the arm, "Parachutes are for cowards, right? Just don't accidentally light us on fire and we'll be fine."

You take to the air before Frank can change his mind. You've got a job to do, and you can't wait for him to decide whether he's afraid or not.

Soon you see the German army below. Frank quickly takes photographs of railroad lines and enemy troops. You do your best to fly as straight and as accurately as possible. When he gives you the OK signal, you turn back. That's when you see the German plane in the distance. It's headed your way.

To fight, turn to page 28.

To try to avoid confrontation, turn to page 39.

Shots ring out as you pass the German pilot. Two bullet holes appear in your wing. You turn the plane and head back to face your foe. Frank seems to have gotten over his fear. He stands up in his seat and fires. A piece of the German airplane breaks off.

"Good shot!" you yell. Frank fires again. The German pilot waves and laughs as the bullet goes wide. He aims his gun at your engine, but his shot misses.

"Have you got a revolver, old boy?" Frank shouts. "My ammunition's all gone." You hand him your gun and he shoots until there are no more bullets. You want to get out of there.

"One more time!" Frank cries. "Get as close as you can!"

To make another pass, turn to page 38.

To go home, turn to page 39.

The reconnaissance planes brought back sketches and photos of enemy positions. You study every line and shadow, trying to memorize which target is which. Your mission is to bomb the railway lines.

At dawn you and the other pilots prepare the planes. You load bombs into the second seat of the plane. It will be just you up there this time.

You've never used bombs on a mission before. When you ask about bomb training, the instructor laughs. "Just toss 'em over the side when you see something worth bombing," he says. "Hopefully you'll hit something."

29

Once in the air, everything on the ground fades away. You're alone and free in the clear dawn sky. When you see the railroad line, you stand up, grab a bomb, and throw it over the side.

Turn the page.

Soon you're out of bombs—and just in time. In the distance several planes zoom and dive like a flock of birds. There's no way to tell which side they're on. One plane bursts into flames and falls out of the sky. Another starts flying toward you. You're out of bombs. All you have left is your revolver and some extra bullets.

The bombs pilots dropped weighed about 20 pounds apiece.

To join the fight, turn to page 41.

To head for the base, turn to page 42.

There are a lot of observers and only so many planes. You'll get your turn eventually. Instead, you get familiar with the wireless radio equipment and Morse code. But the things the wireless operators tell you are dark. They hear everything that goes on. Planes crashing or pilots falling out of the sky are common. One in four practice flights ends in an accident. The idea of flying quickly loses its appeal.

When you get the news your turn is tomorrow, you feel terror. By now you know the planes have a lot of mechanical problems. Most pilots only have a few hours' training before they are cleared for combat. And recon missions are dangerous. Pilots need to fly slowly and in straight lines to allow the photographer to take detailed photographs. But this makes them easy targets. Dozens of pilots and observers have been shot down.

Turn the page.

Later at night when the camp is quiet, you slip away. You've stolen some plain clothes—your uniform would give you away as a deserter.

It's a few miles to the nearest train station, but the darkness will hide you. If you are lucky, you'll be home by suppertime tomorrow. But how will you be received by your friends and family? You may be facing public shame, prison time, or even execution. But at least you're alive for now.

THE END

To follow another path, turn to page 9.

To read the conclusion, turn to page 101.

You like the sound of being a knight—but a knight with two feet on the ground. While James and the mechanic fix the engine, you find the training officer. "I'm not afraid to die for my country," you say, "but I would like to actually be in combat when I go."

"It's your lucky day," the officer says. "Just got orders that an artillery unit needs a new wireless man with them on the ground. Seems their last one got blown up."

As you pack your things, you're oddly relieved. You could be shot, blown up, or hit with poison gas. And someone had to die for this position to open up. It won't be an easy or safe job, but you'd rather die on foot than falling from the sky.

33

THE END

To follow another path, turn to page 9.

To read the conclusion, turn to page 101.

The engine starts with a roar. Soon you and James are rolling and bouncing down the field, going faster and faster. Then you're airborne! The ground shrinks as the plane climbs.

You are too excited to be scared. James circles the field several times as you practice taking pictures and radioing to the ground. It's fun to finally use what you've learned. You give James the thumbs-up so he knows you're finished. He turns the plane toward the landing field.

Suddenly the engine sputters and then dies. It seems to float on air for a moment before tipping nose-first. Then it begins its rapid descent.

"What's going on?" you yell.

"I don't know!" James yells back. You can see him fiddling with the plane's controls. Nothing he does seems to work.

Smoke trails out the back of the plane, leaving a black streak in the sky. The ground spirals closer as you struggle to undo the seat straps in the hopes of being thrown clear of the plane.

When the plane hits, you're tossed out of the cockpit like a rag doll. Your body skips over the rough ground, scraping your skin. Your leather helmet protects the top of your head a little, but your face is bare. Flaming pieces of the plane cartwheel after you. One hits your body and your clothes catch fire.

Many planes were not tested before being sent to Royal Air Force pilots.

Turn the page.

It takes several surgeries to save you. After your body is patched together, you're sent to Dr. Harold Gilles. He specializes in plastic surgery, a new field of medicine. He does a good job, but there's only so much he can do. Your face will never be the same.

Your body may be broken and your face battle scarred, but you are the lucky one. Like too many pilots in the war, James didn't make it. He was only 18 years old.

THE END

36

To follow another path, turn to page 9.

To read the conclusion, turn to page 101.

"Who's next?" the officer asks. No one raises his hand. Most of the men are watching as medics rush to the downed plane. The officer frowns and tries to block their view. "You have to face the risk," he says. "Airplanes have never been used in war. You men will be remembered as the first, the bravest, and the best pilots in the world!"

"Shortest-lived too," the man next to you mumbles. "I heard the average lifespan in the Royal Flying Corps is 11 days."

That's it. Flying isn't for you, and the officer's glare won't change your mind. By the end of the day you have new orders: report to the artillery unit for training. Now instead of flying a plane, you'll be shooting them out of the sky.

THE END

To follow another path, turn to page 9.

To read the conclusion, turn to page 101.

The German plane flies so close the wings of your planes almost touch. Frank throws the gun at the enemy's propeller. It bounces off without doing any damage. The other pilot laughs, salutes, and pulls away.

"That's all I've got!" Frank yells. Quickly you turn for home. The enemy disappears in the opposite direction. You land and Frank delivers the photographs to the commanders planning the battle. You've made it back in time for breakfast. In the mess hall, everyone listens to the story of Frank throwing the gun. You have survived another day as a pilot.

38

THE END

To follow another path, turn to page 9.

To read the conclusion, turn to page 101.

You are not getting involved in a dogfight. The damage to the wing is worse than you thought. Shots are fired, but you can't figure out where the shooter is.

As you spin around to check behind you, Frank's body tips. He slowly slides out of the plane. He tries to grab the wing, but there's nothing to hold onto. You watch in horror for a few seconds before snapping back to attention. You've got to save yourself.

The term "dogfight" was first used during World War I. It refers to a battle in the air fought at close range.

Turn the page.

The German plane disappears. You can make it back, but just barely. The airfield is only a few miles away when the engine sputters, then stalls. You're not going down like this! The controls are frozen but you manage to pull it out of the nosedive just in time for a crash landing.

The other pilots are stunned when you walk away from the burning plane. So are you. You've lived to fight another day. If only Frank were here with you.

THE END

To follow another path, turn to page 9.

To read the conclusion, turn to page 101.

It's a squad of German fighters on the attack. Two Allied planes try to fight them off, but the Germans are faster. Gunfire bursts from one German plane. They have machine guns! You don't have time to wonder how they manage to fly and shoot through the propellers. You swoop, dive, and then shoot your revolver at the nearest German plane. Its engine explodes and it spins crazily as it falls out of the sky.

One enemy down! But the air is full of German planes. One releases a burst of gunfire that takes out your rudder. You're pinned to the seat as your plane twists and spins in the air. There's nothing to do but wait for the end. You hope your fellow pilots will tell your family that you lived your final moments as a hero.

THE END

To follow another path, turn to page 9.

To read the conclusion, turn to page 101.

You've heard that the Germans have a new weapon—mounted machine guns. The Allies tried machine guns in the planes, but the propeller got in the way of the bullets. Somehow the Germans have figured out how to shoot through the propeller.

One of the German planes zooms toward you. Gunfire rips holes in your plane but misses the engine. But then your throttle jams! The ground rushes toward you with alarming speed. The gunfire stops, probably because the German pilot thinks you're already dead.

Another hard push on the throttle, and it gives. Slowly you level out of the dive, making a big curve and missing the ground by just a few hundred feet. You gasp for air as you realize you've been holding your breath.

There's no sign of the German planes, but that doesn't mean they're gone. As your plane climbs, you expect a bullet in the back at any moment. Nothing happens, though. You head for home knowing you just survived a brush with death.

THE END

To follow another path, turn to page 9.

To read the conclusion, turn to page 101.

Shallow trenches were used for firing machine guns, throwing grenades, and observing.

3
BIG GUNS AND
DEEP HOLES

When you enlisted in the army in 1914, everyone thought this was going to be a short war. All your friends joined up right away. It sounded like a great adventure!

No one thought the war would grind on for years. But now both sides have dug in for the long haul. Trenches zigzag across the Western Front, which stretches 440 miles from the North Sea to the border of Switzerland. Soldiers live in the trenches and wait for the order to attack. The Germans are on one side. The Allies are on the other side.

45

Turn the page.

In the middle is an empty area called no-man's-land. In some places, the trenches are less than 45 feet apart—easily within range of a grenade.

No-man's-land is tangled with miles of looped barbed wire and rigged with hundreds of land mines. The mines have torn up the earth, making it a mud pit after rainfall. Anyone sent on an attack or scouting mission must cross this desolate strip. Machine guns and snipers wait on both sides. Here and there, bloated bodies rest unclaimed.

Artillery fire has turned no-man's-land into a crater-filled desert. Neither side seems to want to move. Both sides fire at one another all the time from the trenches. Shells explode above your head every day. Something has to happen soon, or no one will win.

Everyone you knew when you enlisted is dead. Almost all the friends you made in the army are dead. You're not sure how you have managed to survive. You hope your luck will hold out.

To be a soldier in the trenches on the Western Front, turn to page 48.

To be part of a tank crew during the Battle of Passchendaele, turn to page 56.

Trench life is wet, dirty, and crowded. Everyone eats and sleeps in the trenches. Bodies are buried and garbage is thrown right outside. When it rains, refuse is swept back in. There is no safe place to get clean or to use the bathroom.

Water flows right in. Nobody has dry feet, and trench foot, a kind of fungus, is widespread. Sometimes the fungal infection gets so bad that men get gangrene and have to have their feet amputated. The air is filled with the stench of mud, waste, rotten food, and death.

Every week soldiers move to different trenches. The lines at the front are called attack trenches. Behind them are supply trenches filled with men, food, and ammunition. Support trenches filled with emergency supplies lie behind that. Communication trenches connect them all.

The communications trenches made it possible for soldiers at the front line to receive fresh supplies.

The German army is only about a half mile away. Things have been quiet lately. But one day word comes that the Germans are planning to attack.

To join a machine gun crew, turn to page 50.

To assist a trench mortar crew, turn to page 53.

It takes six men to shoot a machine gun. You're the only one left of the original crew. The five raw recruits in front of you look terrified. They should be, you think.

"This gun fires 400 rounds a minute," you say, patting it. "That makes it better than 80 rifles. I'll shoot the gun. Two of you gather ammunition. The others make sure there is plenty of water to keep the gun cool. It gets hot firing so many rounds at once."

One of the recruits, John, has not been paying attention. Before you can reprimand him, he says, "Something strange is coming. It's a sort of greenish yellow cloud rolling toward us."

Poison gas! Gas is a terrible weapon. There are several types, and all are deadly.

Phosgene has a mild odor and spreads rapidly. Phosgene doesn't do much right away, but over a 48-hour period it can poison and kill a healthy soldier. Chlorine enters the respiratory system and attacks the lungs. Mustard gas causes chemical burns inside and outside the body. It can kill and injure thousands of people with just one application. Sometimes the enemy combines the gases to maximize their attack.

Germany launched its first successful gas attack in January 1915. More than 1,000 Russian soldiers were killed.

To grab your gas mask, turn to page 52.

To sound the alarm, turn to page 62.

You've only got about 20 seconds before the gas gets to the trenches. The mask smells terrible and gives you a headache, but it's better than getting poisoned.

You stumble through the gas cloud to the machine gun. The German army is moving forward, using the cloud as cover. You fire into the cloud as fast as the other crewmen can feed the ammunition.

One of the new recruits is hit, then another. You keep firing. There's no way to tell if you're hitting anything, but you keep at it.

52

John is lying over the top of the trench, covered in blood. He has his mask on. He might still be alive.

To try to save John, turn to page 63.

To continue firing, turn to page 65.

Trench mortars are perfect weapons for the trenches. They are short tubes that shoot artillery shells long distances and are very easy to use. All you do is drop the small bomb into the tube. When the bomb hits the bottom of the tube, a firing pin ignites the charge and fires off the rounds. Your gun can shoot up to 22 rounds a minute and hit a target 1,200 yards away. It can also fire over buildings and other structures.

Unlike cannons, mortars fire and land in a high arc. Their rounds could land inside enemy trenches.

Turn the page.

One of the crew brings out a reconnaissance photo of the German line. Several areas are circled in red. Quickly the crew lines up the gun and fires. The crew's dog, Hero, watches calmly from near the top of the trench.

The army uses thousands of dogs to carry messages, move equipment, and even help the injured off the battlefield. Dogs can easily leap over trenches, sniff out mines, find wounded men, and sneak under barbed wire and other obstacles. They are also smaller targets for enemy snipers and can dodge faster than a man.

They also make great guards. If the German army approaches, Hero growls a warning. Not much gets by a trench dog. Hero even has his own gas mask, in case there is an attack.

Suddenly Hero pricks his ears. You look around to see what has caught his attention, but it's too late. A huge explosion throws you backward! A large German mortar round has hit the trench. Bodies fly through the air. A large section of the trench collapses, burying several soldiers in deadly mud. You're trapped in mud to your waist.

To try to escape, turn to page 66.

To stay put, turn to page 67.

Tanks are the new secret weapon of this war. They didn't have a very good start, though. Early tanks were slow. They broke down often. But even the slowest tank is an impressive sight. The huge metal machines can easily climb over enemy trenches, break through barbed wire fences, and defend their crew from bullets. Your tank is much better. It's faster and more reliable.

This is your first mission on a tank crew. The plan is for the tank to attack and destroy several farm buildings taken over by the Germans.

It's going to be rough. Weeks of mortar and machine gun fire churned up the dirt. Then it rained heavily for several days. The mud is so thick and deep that men can drown in it. Even knee-deep mud is a problem—getting stuck on foot presents an easy target for enemy snipers.

It's crowded and cramped inside the tank with six other men. No one can stand fully upright, and a tiny bulb is the only light source. Slowly the tank creeps forward. You go a couple of miles, and then the tank stops.

To try to free the tank, turn to page 58.

To get out to see what's wrong, turn to page 69.

The tank seems to be stuck in mud. Slowly you steer it one way, then the other, and eventually it moves forward again. You're lucky. It doesn't take much to disable a tank. The clumsy machines are easily stopped by mud, ditches, wire, or by getting caught on tree stumps.

Tanks were also called landships.

58

Machine gun fire hits the tank. Most bounces harmlessly off, but a few bullets make it through. One hits the tank driver. He falls onto the throttle. Before you can pull him off, the tank makes a hard lurch forward, driving into a huge mud crater. It falls nose-first into the crater. For a few moments all is quiet. Then you feel the tank sink deeper into the mud.

To send someone outside to look at the damage, turn to page 60.

To go outside and look at the damage yourself, turn to page 71.

"I'll go out," one soldier volunteers. You give him the OK and he disappears. Almost instantly, machine gun fire rains down on the tank. You feel the patter of the shots run down your spine.

You don't have to look outside to know that the soldier is dead, but you wait a moment anyway. When you don't hear anything, you know you are right.

"I volunteer to go out next, sir," another crewman says. He tries to sound brave, but you can hear his voice quiver. You can see he is nursing his arm. Small bits of shrapnel have cut into his skin, and dots of blood are beginning to show through his sleeve. Two of the other men broke bones when the tank hit the crater.

"No," you reply. "We'll try to drive it out."

You restart the tank, thinking the engine's vibrations might help you break free of the mud. Instead, the movement buries it deeper. German mortar fire and machine gun fire explode all around. The tank's guns are useless. One is in the mud, and the other is pointing at the sky.

"Sir," one of the crew gets your attention. "Our side does not know we are still alive in here. If they think the Germans will steal this tank, they'll bomb us too. We're dead either way. I volunteer to go back, sir."

He's right. Someone has to go back and tell the Allies that there are survivors in your tank. "But we'll wait for dark," you decide.

To go back yourself, turn to page 72.
To send the crewman, turn to page 73.

Quickly you bang the alarm bell. Instantly other alarm bells ring out down the line. German bombs explode everywhere. Two of the new recruits fall dead from sniper fire. Your nose and eyes begin to burn, but in the chaos you can't find your gas mask. Frantically you search the area near the machine gun.

Suddenly the nauseating chemical scent of chlorine is in the air. You panic and take several deep breaths in a row. This is a huge mistake, and you fall to the ground, choking and gasping. Two pale green gas clouds wrap around your body. Your eyes, mouth, and throat are on fire. A few minutes later you are dead.

THE END

To follow another path, turn to page 9.

To read the conclusion, turn to page 101.

He's the last friend you have left alive. As you reach for him, a sniper's bullet grazes your arm. You flinch and notice that your exposed hands are starting to burn and blister. Another bullet hits you high in the same arm.

You and James fall into a heap at the bottom of the trench, along with the injured and dead. The last thing you hear before you black out are more explosions and screams.

Half of all British soldiers in the trenches suffered an injury during the war. Poison gas was one of the main causes.

Turn the page.

The next thing you know, you are in a field hospital. You open your eyes to see a smiling woman. Her name tag says Irene Curie. She notices you're awake and says, "Well, hello there! You're lucky to be alive. A strong wind blew the gas out of the trenches. Your mates got you and your friend out."

"Now we have to X-ray that arm," she continues. "My mother, Marie Curie, organized a group of motor-ambulances to bring X-ray machines to the front lines. We'll get you checked out in a minute."

64

John is in the bed beside you. He's pale but alive. You look at each other. The war isn't over. You know you'll be back out there soon.

THE END

To follow another path, turn to page 9.

To read the conclusion, turn to page 101.

Suddenly, your head feels like it's bursting. Your throat goes dry and everything starts to swim. The mask must be leaking! The dead body beside you still has his mask. You grab the dead man's mask, hold your breath, and switch.

A line of figures appears along the top of the trench. You can tell from their uniforms that they are Germans. They're wearing gas masks and carrying long, tubelike weapons you've never seen before. Each soldier also has a large metal tank strapped to his back.

One of them gives a signal. They all lift their weapons and point into the trench. Bursts of flame shoot out, covering everything in the trench. "So that's how a flamethrower works," you think just before you are burned alive.

THE END

To follow another path, turn to page 9.

To read the conclusion, turn to page 101.

You claw at the mud with your hands, trying to free yourself. A terrible sight greets you when you've cleared the mud away. One leg has been shot off. You see it a few feet away. It seems unreal—that can't be part of your body. You don't feel any different. There's no pain. But your eyes tell you that it's real.

"That's it, then," you think. Another explosion rocks the trench. The last thing you see is an avalanche of sand and slimy mud falling on top of you.

THE END

To follow another path, turn to page 9.

To read the conclusion, turn to page 101.

Hero appears through the smoke. "Good dog!" you shout, relieved. You grab his collar and he pulls you out. Another explosion rocks the trench. The Germans must have figured out where the mortar fire was coming from.

Slowly Hero pulls you behind the trench line. That's when you notice the blood on his fur. He's been shot! Once you both are safe, Hero collapses and you black out.

Around 20,000 dogs assisted the Allies on the Western Front.

67

Turn the page.

You wake up in a makeshift field hospital. Hundreds of injured men lie on blankets and gurneys. Hero is on a blanket beside you. His leg is carefully bandaged, but otherwise he looks fine. He licks your hand when you reach out to pet his soft fur. Hero saved your life, and you'll never forget this brave war dog.

THE END

To follow another path, turn to page 9.

To read the conclusion, turn to page 101.

You hop out to see what's going on. A huge mass of barbed wire is trailing behind the tank. The wire must be caught somewhere on its body. The dangerous wire will make it even more difficult to get the tank out of the mud. Several other tanks are trapped in mud as well.

You signal the crew to abandon the tank. As they crawl out, bombs begin to fly in your direction. Everyone tries to run, but they instantly become trapped in the mud themselves.

Artillery shells tore up the ground and created huge waterlogged holes. Thousands of men drowned in the mud pits.

Turn the page.

You're in mud up to your chest and sinking fast. Frantically, you try to climb out, but the movement only covers you with more mud. Your hands become heavy with caked-on mud.

Eventually you are too tired to struggle. You can feel the mud leeching through your clothing, down the back of your shirt, and in your ears. Soon your head disappears beneath the mud forever. Your war has ended.

THE END

To follow another path, turn to page 9.

To read the conclusion, turn to page 101.

Every tank has a special beam that is made to free a tank in situations just like this. You crawl out of the tank and immediately see how bad it is.

Just then the tank is hit with machine gun fire. You try to scramble back inside, but a bullet rips through your leg. Several more follow, pummeling the rest of your body. You slide down the side of the tank and disappear into the mud. You hope your comrades will recover your body. The Allies have lost another soldier.

THE END

To follow another path, turn to page 9.

To read the conclusion, turn to page 101.

You order the healthy soldier to care for the three wounded men while you're away. It's late when you slowly open the tank door and slip out. You manage to avoid the worst of the mud and make it back to the trenches. The officers are shocked at your story. No one can believe that anyone survived. They assure you that the tank won't be bombed as long as the survivors are inside.

It's another day before you can get back to the tank. Everyone is weak and hungry but still alive. Together, you make your way back to the trenches on foot—the vibrations from riding in a tank could further injure those with broken bones. It's a slow, dangerous journey, but you know everyone is glad to be away from the tank.

THE END

To follow another path, turn to page 9.

To read the conclusion, turn to page 101.

72

As soon as darkness falls, the crewman slips away. Some time later there is a loud commotion outside the tank. It's more machine gun fire from the Germans. Suddenly the tank door opens. At first you think it's the crewman returning. Then a hand grenade drops into the tank! Quickly you toss the grenade out. Another crewman shoots the German soldier who threw the grenade.

For another day the Germans mercilessly attack the tank. Your ears ring from the endless sound of bullets bouncing against metal. Gunfire or shrapnel wounds everyone, but no one is dead. Yet. If you're going to escape, now is the time to do it. The wounded men can't wait. If you wait any longer someone will surely die.

"Do you think anyone is coming for us?" one man whispers.

Turn the page.

It's dark inside the tank so you can't see his face, but you can tell he is afraid. You know the other men are waiting for your response.

"No," you say. You feel honesty is best if you're going to survive. "It's up to us to save ourselves."

At nightfall you and your men slip out of the tank. You help support the most injured men until they're firmly on the ground. A moment passes while you all hold your breath, waiting.

No-man's-land near Ypres, France, in 1919

But this time there is no gunfire. You pass the remains of the crewman on the way back. The mine he stepped on didn't leave much behind, but you recognize the pin he wore on his uniform.

The sense of relief you feel when back in the trenches is an odd one. Trench life is no picnic. But you would rather be surrounded by trench foot, lice, and mud than trapped and wounded in a tank.

THE END

To follow another path, turn to page 9.

To read the conclusion, turn to page 101.

The fighting in the Dardanelles began in 1915. The strait in northwestern Turkey separates Europe from Asia.

4
WAR AT
SEA

You've always loved the sea. You dreamed of sailing on the open ocean. You could have joined the Royal Navy as a cadet at 13 or served as a port steward or clerk at 14. But your parents wouldn't let you join until you turned 16. Lucky for you the war has waited for you. You signed up on your birthday, and now you're a sailor—and just in time. Both armies are stuck in a standoff in trenches on land. The only hope for the Allies is a naval victory.

There is only one problem. German submarines called U-boats terrorize the seas. Submarines are one of the newest and most deadly weapons of the Great War.

77

Turn the page.

By the end of the war, German U-boats sank more than 10 million tons of Allied ships and supplies.

German U-boats sneak through the sea, destroying any ship they find. Their main goal is to disrupt ships bringing supplies, weapons, and soldiers to the Allies.

U-boats are far more advanced than any other country's subs. Each can carry 12 torpedoes and stay underwater for two hours at a time.

Before the war is over, Germany's 375 U-boats will be responsible for sinking thousands of military boats, hospital ships, passenger steamers, mine layers, and merchant ships.

Great Britain has its own submarine fleet. They also have another deadly weapon: the dreadnought. Dreadnoughts are superships with more guns and power than any other ship in the world. Each ship is more than 500 feet long and requires a crew of 800.

There is nothing more you want than to blow a German submarine or ship out of the water. Soon you will get your chance.

79

To dive beneath the waves in a British submarine in the Dardanelles, turn to page 80.

To sail the ocean on a battle cruiser at the Battle of Jutland, turn to page 86.

You live in a big metal tube under water. It is stuffy and cramped inside the submarine. No matter how cold it is, you cannot turn on the heat. It would waste electricity. It smells like engine oil and unwashed bodies. There is not enough light to read or write by.

The submarine is underwater during the day. At night it comes to the surface. That's when the batteries get recharged and everyone gets some fresh air. You like to walk along the top of the sub at night, breathing in the salt air.

This mission has been to patrol the coast and watch for enemy ships. Early one morning you are assigned periscope duty. "Today is going to be a good day," you think as a ship appears in your viewfinder.

To get a closer look, go to page 81.

To follow it at a distance, turn to page 83.

The sub dives quickly. The torpedo crew gets the ammunition ready. Your sub has four torpedo tubes. It is the most powerful sub in the Royal Navy.

It has been a while since you have come across an enemy ship. It will be exciting to get to use the torpedoes again.

Submarines were the first British naval force called to action and the last to return to port after the war was over.

Turn the page.

When the sub gets closer to the ship, it is time to resurface and release the torpedo. This is the most dangerous time for the submarine. If it's a German ship, it will fire. The sub might not have enough time to dive and get away. But this might be an Allied ship or a merchant ship carrying food and supplies.

You take another look through the periscope. It is the familiar sight of guns and turrets of a British battle ship.

To resurface, turn to page 89.

To stay underwater and move past the ship, turn to page 90.

It could be a merchant ship. But it could
be a German or Allied battleship too. There's
risk even if it is a British ship. They often shoot
submarines on sight, unless they are completely
sure the sub is not German. You have heard of
many British submarine crews blown up by their
own ships.

The sub surfaces again and you take another
look. Yes, it is a British battleship. There is no
reason to get any closer, so the commanding
officer orders the sub to dive and continue on.

That evening the officer tells the crew that
you have new orders. The Allies are about
to launch an attack against the enemy in the
Dardanelles in northwestern Turkey.

83

Turn the page.

Winston Churchill, First Lord of the Admiralty, who commands the Royal Navy, and other Allied commanders are desperate to end this war. Turkey is fighting for the Germans. Your commanders are hoping to defeat the Turkish army. Your orders are to destroy Turkish ships.

You arrive in the middle of the night. You hear that Turkish forces have been destroying Allied ships and subs.

Unpredictable weather and strong currents have given the Dardanelles Strait a reputation as one of the most hazardous waterways in the world.

You have to move through the Dardanelles. This narrow channel has been thought of as an important area throughout the war. It separates Europe from Asia. Most of the strait is several miles wide, but in some places it is less than 4,800 feet across.

Slowly your submarine creeps along the surface through the heavily guarded strait. Suddenly, the world is bright. Searchlights shine directly on your submarine. An enemy patrol ship is almost on top of you.

To fire on the ship, turn to page 92.

To dive, turn to page 94.

The huge metal battle cruiser HMS *Queen Mary* hums beneath your feet. She is outfitted with the most modern weapons in the world. Her 13.5-inch guns were built in secret and are larger and more accurate than any other.

The *Queen Mary* can shoot torpedoes, and she has special antiaircraft guns too. She's also the fastest battleship ever built. You are part of the gunnery crew that fires the weapons. You're ready to shoot some German ships.

It looks like you are about to get your wish. The Royal Navy's fleet is rushing to battle in the North Sea, off the Jutland Peninsula of Denmark. In the distance you see what you've been waiting for: the German fleet.

It will be a huge naval battle. Altogether there are 250 ships and 100,000 sailors ready to test their skills at sea.

An order is given: "Load all guns!" You jump onto the forward turret, the platform on which the gun is mounted, and aim the gun at the German ships. You're ready to fire when the command comes. A huge blast shakes the turret as the gun goes off. Smoke and fire fill the air. You fire again. It looks like one of the enemy ships is hit!

"This is a great game!" you shout. "First blood to *Queen Mary!*"

The HMS *Queen Mary* was more than 700 feet long and had a crew of more than 1,000.

Turn the page.

As you turn to fire again, a huge explosion rocks your ship. Pieces of turret fly through the air, showering the neighboring ship, the HMS *Tiger*, with the wreckage. The gunnery crew falls as a second shock comes.

The ship is listing badly. One side of the ship is rising out of the water, while the other side begins to sink. Men are climbing ladders to get to the dry side. There is a large crowd already there, and no one wants to move.

"Don't worry, men!" an officer says. "She'll float for a long time. We're safe here." But you have a bad feeling.

To stay on the ship, turn to page 96.

To take your chances in the water, turn to page 98.

The officer orders someone to go out onto the submarine and give a signal. This will tell the ship's crew that you are not an enemy submarine. The sailor disappears up the ladder.

A huge explosion rocks the submarine. The battleship has fired at you! The officer curses and barks the order to dive. Another explosion rips a hole in the submarine near the torpedo tubes. The submarine explodes, sending you and the rest of the crew to watery deaths by friendly fire.

THE END

To follow another path, turn to page 9.

To read the conclusion, turn to page 101.

There is no need to alarm the battle ship by surfacing. Down, down, you go, and soon the ship is far behind. When you get off duty you go to your narrow bunk. Just as you doze off, an alarm echoes through the sub. Then an explosion throws you out onto the floor.

"It's a mine!" someone shouts.

The Turkish navy laid 324 mines across the Dardanelles Strait.

Special German U-boats plant explosives throughout the water where Allied ships and submarines are likely to go. The mines are suspended in the water on a cable, floating serenely until ships or submarines disturb them. Submarines like yours.

Cold ocean water pours into your bunk so fast that you do not have time to escape. The submarine sinks to the bottom of the ocean with you and the rest of the crew inside.

THE END

To follow another path, turn to page 9.

To read the conclusion, turn to page 101.

It's almost too late when the order comes. "Fire torpedoes!" You rush to obey. At least you don't have to worry about accuracy at this close range. The patrol ship seems almost too close. It looks enormous through the periscope.

The torpedo fires true. You can see the trail of bubbles in its wake as it zips toward the enemy. Then the patrol ship explodes in a fiery ball. The impact nearly sweeps you off your feet, and you have to grip the periscope handles to stay upright.

You look through the periscope just as a huge column of water more than 600 feet high shoots straight in the air. You can see the patrol ship's crew dashing around the deck as it begins to list dangerously on its side. Some of the lifeboats cannot be lowered because the boat is tilted too much. Several men jump right into the ocean to save themselves.

But the other patrol boats don't sit idly by. They answer your torpedo shot with a rain of gunfire. Their guns take out your periscope and part of the submarine's engine. There is no way to dive or fire again. You're dead in the water. The smell of diesel fuel fills your nose.

Soon you hear clanking above your head as the enemy prepares to board. Turkish soldiers enter the submarine and handcuff everyone. You're marched onto their patrol boat. You are now a prisoner of war.

THE END

To follow another path, turn to page 9.

To read the conclusion, turn to page 101.

"Dive!" the officer shouts. The water distorts your position and the patrol boat's aim is off. Gunfire skips off the ocean's surface and you disappear beneath the waves unharmed. Mines dot the water's surface, but you manage to dive below them. By sunrise you know you're safe.

For the next few days your crew sails at periscope depth, searching for enemy ships. Your job is to look through the periscope, which sticks up about five feet from the ocean's surface. When you see something, your job is to report its position. Then the submarine dives and fires.

It's exciting—after the torpedoes are released, the sub resurfaces and you watch the explosions. You'll never forget the burst of water and cloud of smoke that tells you the torpedo has hit its target. Everyone on the sub can feel the vibrations in the water after a successful sinking.

The crew sinks several ships, including a transport, two ammunition ships, and a gunboat. When you run out of torpedoes, the sub sneaks back out the straits to the Allied forces. Maybe you will get a medal for this one day. For now you are happy the mission was successful and that you lived through it.

THE END

To follow another path, turn to page 9.

To read the conclusion, turn to page 101.

The British had more than 6,600 casualties at the Battle of Jutland. German losses numbered more than 3,000.

He's probably right. The ship isn't going to sink. You barely have time to think that when several new explosions tear through the ship. One hits the area under the left turret, starting a fire and filling it with smoke and gas. An order is given to evacuate the area. You're trying to help a wounded man as another explosion shakes the ship. Men and debris fly through the air.

You find yourself in the water. It's hard to see. Fuel oil and salt water burn your eyes. You flail your arms and try to swim away from the huge ship, which is now sinking quickly. A piece of the ship flies through the air and strikes you in the head. You go down with the ship.

THE END

To follow another path, turn to page 9.

To read the conclusion, turn to page 101.

"Who's going in with me?" you shout. A few men follow you into the water. You swim away from the ship as fast as you can. You are only about 50 yards out when there is another terrific explosion. Huge pieces of metal crash into the water around you. You dive under to avoid getting hit, but suddenly the water seems to suck you away.

"The ship is sinking and it's taking me with it!" you think. Something bumps against you. You grab it, and it carries you to the surface. The breath you take fills your lungs with sweet, fresh air before you pass out.

You wake up covered in oil, floating on a piece of splintery wood, and surrounded by the debris of the *Queen Mary*. Someone throws a rope and pulls you onto a boat.

"Are you German or English?" he asks. You tell him you are part of the crew of the *Queen Mary*.

"You were a part of its crew," he corrects you sadly.

Only eight others survived. You spend the rest of your life wondering how such a huge ship could have gone down so easily and why you were spared while others lost their lives.

THE END

To follow another path, turn to page 9.

To read the conclusion, turn to page 101.

Gas was one of the most feared attacks. Anyone unable to put his mask on in time suffered for days or weeks before finally dying.

5

FUTURE
OF WAR

The United States joined the war in 1917. By the time the war ended in 1918, more than 37 million people were dead, wounded, or missing, including 323,000 American soldiers. The world was shocked at how terrible war had become.

Before this war most fighting was done face to face. Soldiers fought hand to hand or shot their enemies at close range. The modern weapons of the Great War changed that. For the first time, people could kill each other in large numbers across long distances on land, from the air, and across the sea.

Some weapons were so terrifying that they have been outlawed forever. Poison gas was especially horrifying. More than 1 million men were killed or wounded by gas attacks in World War I. In 1925 the use of poison gas and other chemical weapons was banned worldwide.

When the Great War began, airplanes were fragile machines made of cloth, wood, and wire. At first both sides only used them for reconnaissance. But in 1915 the Germans developed a system of synchronizing the firing of machine guns with the rotation of the plane's propeller. This system protected the propeller from the bullets.

By the end of the war, deadly fighter planes equipped with machine guns were filling the skies. Their guns could fire between 400 and 1,000 shots per minute.

On the ground tanks were the new weapon of choice. They could crash through barbed wire and crush trenches. Enemy fire bounced off the tanks' metal sides, protecting the men inside.

Both sides had new guns and artillery that killed with ease. Machine guns could take out whole lines of soldiers from a distance. At the Battle of the Somme, German machine gun and artillery fire killed and wounded more than 60,000 British soldiers in one day.

The French and British built more than 6,500 tanks by the end of the war.

Submarines and deadly torpedoes were new inventions that killed without warning. They forced both sides to invent new technologies such as underwater explosives. Warships got bigger, faster, and more powerful. Speedy dreadnoughts were protected by armor and were equipped with antiaircraft guns and torpedoes. They used the new technology of radio for fast and easy communication.

The Battle of Jutland was the largest naval battle of World War I.

More than 8.5 million soldiers fought and died on both sides of World War I. Even more civilians perished. No matter which side they were on, they shared a common experience: the risk of death or serious injury by these terrible new weapons.

TIMELINE

June 28, 1914—Archduke Franz Ferdinand is assassinated.

July 28, 1914—Austria-Hungary declares war on Serbia. The other nations of Europe take sides, which sparks World War I.

August 3, 1914—Germany declares war on France.

August 4, 1914—Germany invades Belgium. Great Britain enters the war to protect Belgium.

September 15, 1914—First trenches are dug along the Western Front.

October 19, 1914—First Battle of Ypres begins trench warfare on the Western Front. The Allies are victorious.

January 19, 1915—First German zeppelin attack on Great Britain. Two people are killed and 16 are injured.

January 31, 1915—Chemical warfare used for the first time by the German army.

February 19, 1915—Battle of the Dardanelles begins and will result in an Allied loss.

May 7, 1915—German U-boat sinks the RMS *Lusitania*.

June 30, 1915—First noted use of flamethrowers by German soldiers.

September 25, 1915—British attack with gas for the first time. Changing winds cause it to backfire, resulting in 60,000 casualties.

February 21–December 18, 1916—The Battle of Verdun is fought. It is the longest battle of the war and results in 1 million casualties.

May 31, 1916—Battle of Jutland; the British lose more men and ships but are able to stop the German navy.

July 1–November 18, 1916—Battle of the Somme is fought on the Western Front. Casualties number around 1 million.

September 15, 1916—British tanks used for the first time at the Battle of the Somme.

April 6, 1917—The United States enters the war.

May 18, 1917—The United States passes the Selective Service Act. The act requires all men between the ages of 21 and 30 to register for military service.

November 20, 1917—The Battle of Cambrai begins; tanks are used in large numbers for the first time.

November 9, 1918—Kaiser Wilhelm II, the last German emperor, gives up his power and flees the country. Later that month Germany forms a new republic.

November 11, 1918—World War I unofficially ends.

June 28, 1919—World War I officially ends when the Treaty of Versailles is signed.

OTHER PATHS TO EXPLORE

In this book you've seen battles from several points of view. Perspectives on history are as varied as the people who lived it. Seeing history from many points of view is an important part of understanding it.

Here are some ideas for other World War I points of view to explore:

1. Airplanes were a new invention at the start of World War I. By the end they had become faster and more powerful war machines. How might air battles have changed over time? (Key Ideas and Details)

2. Allied soldiers came from as far away as Canada, the United States, New Zealand, and South Africa. How would their war experiences have been different from European soldiers? (Integration of Knowledge and Ideas)

3. Tanks, planes, and submarines were not the only new war weapons. Machine guns, poison gas, and hand grenades were also introduced. How did these new technologies change the way war was fought? (Integration of Knowledge and Ideas)

READ MORE

Eldridge, Jim. *50 Things You Should Know About the First World War.* Irvine, Calif.: QEB Publishing, 2014.

Hepplewhite, Peter. *True Stories From World War I.* New York: Macmillan Children's Books, 2014.

Rasmussen, R. Kent. *World War I For Kids: A History with 21 Activities.* Chicago: Chicago Review Press, 2014.

Swain, Gwenyth. *World War I: An Interactive History Adventure.* North Mankato, Minn.: Capstone Press, 2012.

INTERNET SITES

Use FactHound to find Internet sites related to this book. All of the sites on FactHound have been researched by our staff.

Here's all you do:
Visit *www.facthound.com*
Type in this code: 9781491421512

GLOSSARY

artillery (ar-TI-luhr-ee)—cannons and other large guns used during battles

assassinate (us-SASS-uh-nate)—to murder a person who is well known or important

aviation (AY-ve-ay-shun)—the flying or operating of airplanes, helicopters, or other flying machines

cadet (kuh-DET)—a military student

deserter (di-ZURT-ur)—a military member who leaves duty without permission

enlist (in-LIST)—to voluntarily join a branch of the military

flamethrower (FLAYM-throh-uhr)—a weapon that shoots a stream of burning liquid

gangrene (GANG-green)—a condition that occurs when flesh decays

mortar (MOR-tur)—a short cannon that fires shells or rockets high in the air

periscope (PER-uh-skope)—a viewing device with mirrors at each end

reconnaissance (ree-KAH-nuh-suhnss)—a mission to gather information about an enemy

recruit (ri-KROOT)—a new member of the armed forces

shell (SHEL)—a large bullet fired from a cannon

shrapnel (SHRAP-huhl)—pieces that have broken off from an explosive shell

strait (STRAYT)—a narrow waterway connecting two large bodies of water

turret (TUR-it)—a rotating, armored structure that holds a weapon on top of a military vehicle

zeppelin (ZEP-lin)—a large oval-shaped airship with a rigid frame; zeppelins are named for their inventor, Count Ferdinand von Zeppelin

BIBLIOGRAPHY

Bingham, Hiram. *An Explorer in the Air Service*. New Haven, Conn.: Yale University Press, 1920.

Bowyer, Chaz. *History of the RAF*. New York: Hamlyn, 1977.

First World War Flying Training—Taking Flight. Royal Air Force Museum. 12 July 2014. www.rafmuseum.org.uk/research/online-exhibitions/taking-flight/historical-periods/first-world-war-flying-training.aspx

The First World War: Sources For History. The National Archives. 22 July 2014. www.nationalarchives.gov.uk/pathways/firstworldwar/index.htm

Into the Blue: Pilot Training in Canada, 1917–18. Canadian War Museum. 15 July 2014. www.warmuseum.ca/education/online-educational-resources/dispatches/into-the-blue-pilot-training-in-canada-1917-18/

McCartney, Innes. *British Submarines of World War I*. Oxford: Osprey, 2008.

Messimer, Dwight R. *Verschollen: World War I U-Boat Losses*. Annapolis, Md.: Naval Institute Press, 2002.

Sims, William Sowden. *The Victory At Sea*. Fairfield, Calif.: James Stevenson Publisher, 2002.

World War One At Home: War at Sea. BBC. 4 Aug. 2014. www. bbc.co.uk/programmes/p01p32w3

WWI Training. National Museum of the US Air Force. 9 July 2014. www.nationalmuseum.af.mil/factsheets/factsheet.asp?id=683

INDEX